Epoxy Resin Art for Beginners

Step-by-Step Guide: How to Create an Epoxy Resin Masterpiece and Monetize Your Art

TABLE OF CONTENTS

INTRODUCTION

"Arts is the only way to run away without leaving home." – Twyla Tharp

This quote perfectly summarizes the essence of epoxy resin art, a medium that allows you to escape into a world of creativity right from your own space.

Epoxy resin art is a creative discipline that merges artistic expression with the chemical properties of epoxy resin. Epoxy resin itself is a synthetic material composed of epoxy resin and a hardening agent, which, when combined undergo a chemical reaction to produce a solid, durable, and glossy finish.

Artists use the distinctive features of epoxy resin to create intricate and visually striking pieces that vary across different artistic forms.

The root of epoxy resin art can be traced back to the early 20th century when developers initially created epoxy resins for industrial purposes. Industries like aerospace and marine engineering adopted epoxy resin for its exceptional adhesive and protective qualities. However, it was later that creative minds recognized its artistic potential and began experimenting with it.

Today, epoxy resin art has experienced a remarkable resurgence of popularity. It has become a prominent feature in the modern art scene and the DIY crafting world alike. Artists and hobbyists are drawn to epoxy resin for its ability to create glass-like finishes, vivid colors, and captivating depth. Whether you are interested in crafting stunning jewelry, designing unique furniture pieces, or exploring abstract painting techniques, epoxy resin provides a versatile and exciting medium to realize your artistic versions.

This book is designed to introduce beginners to the world of epoxy resin art. It will guide you through the basics of working with resin, from selecting the right type to understand the mixing and curing process. The chapters that follow will provide step-by-step instructions for various projects, tips to achieve the best results, and solutions for common problems.

By the end of this book, you will have a solid understanding of how to create your own resin art pieces, and perhaps even develop your unique style in this versatile and exciting medium.

CHAPTER 1: Understanding Epoxy Resin

Understanding epoxy resin is crucial for any artist or DIY enthusiast as there are several types. Each type offers unique properties and benefits making certain resins more suitable for specific projects. This knowledge allows you to choose the right epoxy resin for your artistic vision, thus ensuring the best results for creations.

In this chapter, we will explore types of epoxy resin, their properties, and the essential tools needed to begin your artistic journey.

Types of Epoxy Resin

Standard epoxy resin is the most common type and ideal for beginners. It strikes a perfect balance between strength, clarity and flexibility, thus making it suitable for a wide range of applications, including small-scale projects like jewelry, coasters, and basic art pieces. The curing time for standard epoxy resin varies, but it generally allows for some working flexibility, which is beneficial for those just starting out with resin art.

UV-Resistant epoxy has been specifically formulated to resist the yellowing effects of ultraviolet light. This type of epoxy is best suited for projects that will be exposed to sunlight, such as outdoor furniture or window displays. Its primary benefit is the prolonged clarity and color integrity of the projects which safeguards them against the fading effects of sunlight.

Food-Safe epoxy is a unique type of epoxy that is certified safe for contact with food once it is fully cured. This makes it an excellent choice for kitchenware projects, such as countertops, cutting boards, and coasters. However, it is important to ensure that the resin is fully cured before using it for any food-related purposes.

Flexible epoxy resin is designed to be more pliable than the standard type, thus making it less prone to cracking under stress. This makes it ideal for projects that require a degree of flexibility, like silicone molds or wearable art. While flexible epoxy may not be as durable or resistant to heat and chemicals as more rigid types, its versatility makes it a popular choice for specific creative applications.

High-Viscosity epoxy is characterized by its thicker consistency, which makes it suitable for creating high-build coatings and dimensional art. It is particularly useful for projects that require a thicker layer of resin, such as encapsulations or large-scale art installations. Working with high-viscosity epoxy requires more careful handling to ensure even spreading and to avoid air bubbles.

Quick-Curing epoxy is designed to cure much faster than standard epoxies. This is particularly useful for time-sensitive projects or for quickly securing elements in place. Depending on the product, quick-curing epoxy can set in a matter of minutes to hours, which makes it a valuable tool in a resin artist's arsenal.

Color epoxy is either pre-tinted or specially formulated to be mixed with pigments for vibrant colors. This type of epoxy is ideal for artistic projects where color is a central element. Precise measurements are required when mixing color epoxy to maintain consistency and ensure proper curing properties.

Properties and Safety measures

Let's now checkout the properties of epoxy resin that make it an appealing medium for artists and craftsmen, followed by crucial safety measures to ensure a safe and enjoyable experience.

Properties:

- **Durability:** Epoxy resin is known for its strength and resistance to wear and tear.
- **Adhesiveness:** It can bound a wide range of materials, making it versatile.
- **Chemical Resistance:** Resistant to many chemicals, making it durable in varied environments.

- **Transparency and Gloss:** It offers a clear, glossy finish, enhancing the aesthetics of your artwork.

Safety Measures:

- **Ventilation:** Always work in a well-ventilated area to avoid inhaling fumes.
- **Protective Gear:** Use gloves, goggles, and masks for safety.
- **Skin Contact:** Avoid direct skin contact and know how to react in case of accidental exposure.
- **Curing Time:** Be aware of the curing time and potential heat generation

Tool and Material Needed

As a beginner, you must have knowledge about the essential tools and materials required for working with epoxy resin. Having the right equipment not only simplifies the process but also ensures the quality and safety of your resin art projects.

Basic Tools:

- Mixing cups and stir sticks for preparing and mixing the resin.

- Measuring tools as accurate measurements are crucial for the resin to cure properly.
- Protective gear, such as gloves, masks, and eyewear.

Application tools:

- Brushes and spatulas for applying and spreading the resin.
- Heat gun or torch to remove air bubbles for a smooth finish.

Additional Materials:

- Colorants and pigments to add color to your resin creations.
- Molds: various shapes and sizes for casting.
- Decorative elements, such as glitter, beads, or dried flowers for embellishment.

CHAPTER 2: Basic Techniques and Tips

In this chapter, we will cover the foundational techniques and tips that are essential for beginners in epoxy resin art. These techniques form the core of resin art creation, ensuring that even first-time artists can achieve impressive results.

Mixing and Pouring Techniques

In epoxy resin art, the process of mixing and pouring is a much an art as it is a science. Understanding and mastering these techniques is essential for achieving desired results. Here is a closer look at each step.

Proper Ratios: The foundation of successful epoxy resin art lies in getting the resin-to-hardener ratio right. It is crucial to meticulously follow the manufacturer's instructions for the specific epoxy resin product you are using. These instructions provide the correct proportions needed for a successful cure. Deviating from these ratios can result in issues with curing, consequently leaving your artwork less than perfect.

Thorough Mixing: After measuring the appropriate amounts of resin and hardener, thorough mixing is the next critical step. To achieve a uniform consistency, which is vital for the curing process, combine the two components meticulously. Avoid rushing this step; patience is key. Mixing too quickly can introduce excess air bubbles, which can negatively impact the final appearance of your resin art. Slow and steady mixing ensures that the resin and hardener are fully blended without excessive bubbling.

Gradual Pouring: When it is time to pour the mixed resin onto your artwork or into molds, take a deliberate and measured approach. Pour the resin slowly and steadily, allowing you to control the flow and minimize the formation of bubbles. The technique is especially crucial when working on intricate or detailed pieces where bubble formation can be more challenging to manage. A gradual pour not only reduces the chances of air entrapment but also gives you more control over the resin's distribution.

Color Mixing and Adding Inclusions

The use of color and inclusions in epoxy resin art not only adds depth and character to the artwork but also allows for personalization and uniqueness in each piece.

Colorants and Pigments

The process of choosing the right colors and promotions is crucial in epoxy resin art. Adding colorant and pigments transforms the clear resin into a vibrant medium, but it is important to use resin-specific colorants or compatible pigments to avoid any adverse chemical reactions. The intensity of the color can be controlled by the amount of pigment added. A small quantity can produce a translucent tint, while more pigment leads to an opaque color. It is essential to add colorants gradually to achieve the desired shade.

Testing colors

Before committing the color to your entire batch of resin, it is advisable to test small quantities. This step is crucial as it allows artists to adjust the hue and intensity, as needed, without waiting materials. Additionally, a test batch provides a better idea of how the color will look once the resin has cured, which can sometimes differ from the wet mix.

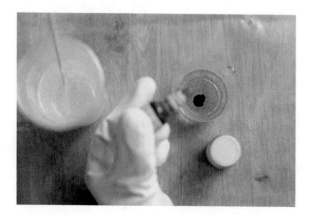

Adding Inclusions

Inclusions such as glitter, beads, or dried flowers can significantly enhance the visual appeal of resin art, by adding texture and interest. It is important to ensure that these inclusions are compatible with the resin and to add them at the appropriate time during the curing process. Some inclusions work best when added while the resin is still liquid, while others are more effective when placed after the resin has started to gel. This careful integration of colors and inclusions plays a pivotal role in creating unique and personalized resin artwork.

Avoiding Bubbles and Ensuring a Smooth Finish

Achieving a bubble-free and smooth finish is a hallmark of high-quality resin art, and it requires careful attention to detail throughout the process.

Removing Bubbles

The presence of bubbles is a common challenge in resin art, but there are effective techniques for their removal. After pouring the resin, you might notice bubbles rising to the surface. A reliable method to remove these bubbles is by using a heat gun or torch. Gently passing the heat tool over the surface helps to pop the bubbles. However, it is crucial to use the heat tool with caution. Overheating can cause the resin to yellow or distort, adversely affecting the final appearance.

Ensuring a Level and Smooth Cure

Preparing a level working surface is essential before starting the pouring process. An uneven surface can cause the resin to pool in certain areas, resulting in an uneven finish. This can significantly detract from the aesthetic quality of the art piece.

The environment in which the resin cures plays a critical role in achieving a flawless finish. It is important to keep the curing area dust free and maintain a consistent temperature as recommended by the resin manufacturer. Variations in temperature and humidity can affect the curing time and the quality of the finish. Controlling these environmental factors ensures a consistent and flawless outcome.

CHAPTER 3: Simple Projects for Beginners

This chapter is dedicated to beginners, offering simple, yet satisfying, projects that are effective for honing your skills. These projects are designed to build confidence and provide a foundation in basic techniques.

Creating Coasters and Trinket Dishes

Creating coasters and trinket dishes with epoxy resin is a perfect project for beginners, combining ease of creation with practicality and artistic expression.

Step 1: Choosing Molds and Preparing Materials

The first step is to select molds that suit your style. This can range from simple circles for coasters to more intricate shapes for trinket dishes. Gather all necessary materials, including epoxy resin, hardener, colorants, and any decorative items you wish to embed, such as glitter or small charms.

Step 2: Mixing and pouring Resin

Prepare the resin according to the manufacturer's instructions, being mindful of the correct ratios and mixing techniques to avoid bubbles. If you're adding colors, mix them in thoroughly until you achieve the desired hue. Pour the resin slowly into the molds, ensuring an even distribution. At this stage, you can add your chosen inclusions, carefully placing them into the liquid resin.

Step 3: Curing and Finishing Touches

Once poured, leave the resin to cure as per the specified time. This can vary depending on the type and brand of resin you are using. After curing, carefully demold your creations. You might need to sand the edges for a smoother finish.

Design Variations and Customization

Coasters and trinket dishes offer a canvas for creativity. Experiment with different color patterns, such as swirling techniques for a marbled effect or layering for depth. Embedding objects like dried flowers or leaves can add a natural, aesthetic appeal.

Practical Uses and Gifting

Not only do these resin creations serve practical uses in your home, but they also make thoughtful, handmade gifts. Customizing them to suit the recipient's taste adds a personal touch that cannot be replicated with store-bought items.

Through creating coasters and trinket dishes, you will gain fundamental skills in resin art, such as mixing, pouring, and curing, which are essential for more advanced projects. This project is a great starting point for exploring the versatile and rewarding world of epoxy resin crafting.

Making Jewelry: Pendants and earrings

Making jewelry, such as pendants and earrings, with epoxy resin is an exciting and creative way to delve into the world of resin crafting. The process allows for a wide range of customization and can produce truly unique, handcrafted items.

1. **Design and Planning:** Begin by deciding on the design for your pendants and earrings. This can range from simple geometric shapes to more elaborate forms. Consider the size, thickness, and whether you want to include inclusions like glitter, color swirls, or small objects like dried flowers, coins, decorative keys, etc.

2. **Selecting Molds and Materials**: Choose silicone molds that match your desired design. Alongside the resin and hardener, gather materials like colorants, hooks for earrings, and decorative elements you wish to include.

3. **Mixing and Pouring**: After preparing your resin mix according to the manufacturer's guidelines, carefully pour it into your molds. If you are adding colors or effects, this is the time to do it. Be mindful of the amount of resin you pour, as jewelry pieces typically require a thinner layer compared to other resin projects.

4. **Adding Inclusions and Embeddings:** If you plan to embed items within your jewelry, carefully place them into the liquid resin. This could be anything from a sprinkle of glitter to a small pressed flower. Ensure they are fully encapsulated by the resin.

5. **Curing and assembly:** After pouring, let the resin cure completely. The time for this can vary, so it is important to follow the specific instructions for the resin you are using. Once cured, demold your creations. You may need to sand the edges for a smooth finish. Attach the hardware, such as earring hooks or pendant bails, to complete your jewelry pieces.

6. **Finishing Touches:** For a professional look, consider adding a clear coat for extra gloss or polishing the pieces with a soft cloth.

Creating resin jewelry is not only a fun and rewarding hobby but also offers the opportunity to make personalized accessories for yourself or bespoke gifts for others. The skills learned in this project, like precision pouring and embedding objects, are foundational for more advanced resin art projects.

Crafting Small Art Pieces

- **Idea Generation:** Start by brainstorming ideas for your small art pieces. Think about themes, color, and what emotions or messages you want to convey. Consider abstract design, miniature landscapes, or representational motifs.

- **Materials Preparation:** Gather all necessary materials, including epoxy resin, hardener, colorants, molds or surfaces to work on (like small canvases or wood pieces), and any decorative elements like glitter or beads.
- **Design Sketching:** Sketch your design ideas on paper first. This helps in visualizing the final piece and serves as a reference during the crafting process.
- **Mixing resin:** Carefully measure and mix the resin and hardener, following the manufacturer's instructions to ensure proper curing.
- **Color and Inclusion Addition:** Add color, glitters, or other inclusions into your resin mix if desired. Experiment with different techniques like swirling, layering, or creating gradients for unique effects.
- **Pouring and Manipulating Resin:** Pour the resin into your chosen surface or into the mold. Use tools like toothpicks, brushes, or blow dryers to manipulate the resin into your desired design.

- **Curing and Monitoring:** Allow the resin to cure in a dust-free temperature-controlled environment. Monitor the curing process to ensure that the resin sets correctly without any unwanted bubbles or imperfections.
- **Demolding and Finishing Touches:** Once fully cured, carefully demold your artwork. Finish the edges with sanding, if necessary, and add any additional paint or varnish for protection and enhanced aesthetics.
- **Display Preparation:** Attach hanging hardware or prepare stands if your art piece is intended for display.
- **Reflection and Learning:** After completing your project, reflect on what techniques worked well and what could be improved for future projects. Each piece is a learning experience in the versatile world of resin art.

CHAPTER 4: Advanced Epoxy Resin Techniques

Epoxy resin art has evolved significantly in recent years, opening up a world of possibilities for artists seeking to push the boundaries of their creativity. In this chapter, we will delve into some advanced epoxy resin techniques that will take your art to the next level.

Layering and 3D Effects

One of the most captivating aspects of epoxy resin art is its ability to create mesmerizing depth and dimensionality. By mastering layering and 3D effects, you can make your artwork come alive.

1. **Creating depth:** Layering epoxy resin allows you to build depth within your artwork. Start by pouring a thin layer of resin onto your surface and allowing it to partially cure. Then, add another layer with your desired colors and elements. You can repeat this process multiple times to achieve a sense of depth that draws viewers into your artwork.

2. **3D Resin Effects:** To take it a step further, experiment with 3D effects. Embed objects, such as shells,

gemstones, or even miniature sculptures, into your resin layers. As you pour additional layers over these objects, they become encapsulated within the artwork, creating a stunning three-dimensional effect.

Incorporating Different Media

Epoxy resin is incredibly versatile and can be combined with various other media to add texture, contrast, and unique character to your artwork. Here are some ways to incorporate different media into your resin creations:

1. **Wood:** Integrating wood into epoxy resin pieces can yield a harmonious blend of natural and synthetic elements. Create river tables by encasing pieces of live-edge wood with resin, or use wood slices as a canvas for your resin artwork. The contrast between the organic wood and the glossy resin can be visually striking.

2. **Glass:** Mixing glass and resin can result in a beautiful fusion of transparency and depth. Consider embedding stained glass shards, colored glass beads, or even

shattered tempered glass into your epoxy resin creations. The interplay of light and texture can produce truly captivating effects.

3. **Metal:** Experiment with metallic elements like copper or aluminum flakes to introduce a shimmering, metallic luster to your epoxy resin artwork. These materials can be mixed into the resin or applied accents on the surface, adding a touch of elegance and contrast.

Creating Large-Scale Artwork

Epoxy resin is not limited to small-scale creations; it can be used to craft stunning large-scale artworks. However, working on a larger canvas comes with its own set of challenges and considerations:

1. **Planning and Preparation:** Before embarking on a large-scale project, meticulously plan your design and gather all necessary materials. Ensure you have a suitable workplace with adequate ventilation and a level surface to accommodate the size of your artwork

2. **Mixing and Pouring:** Mixing larger quantities of epoxy resin requires precision and speed. It is essential to follow the manufacturer's instructions for mixing ratios and working time. Consider enlisting the help of assistants to ensure an even and efficient pour.

3. **Support and curing:** Large resin artworks may require additional structural support to prevent sagging or warping during the curing

process. Utilize braces or molds as needed to maintain the desired shape and thickness.

4.

CHAPTER 5: Finishing and Preservation

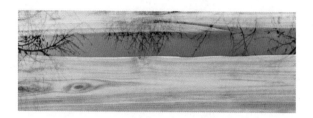

In the world of epoxy resin art, achieving a captivating finish and ensuring the preservation of your artwork are essential steps in creating lasting beauty. In this chapter, we will explore the crucial aspects of finishing and preserving your epoxy resin creations.

Sanding and Polishing

A flawless finish begins with proper sanding and polishing techniques. These steps not only enhance the visual appeal of your artwork but also contribute to its tactile quality.

1. **Sanding:** After your epoxy resin has fully cured, it may have imperfections, such as bubbles, rough patches, or uneven surfaces. Start the finishing process by sanding your artwork. Begin with lower grit sandpaper (e.g. 120-220) to remove major imperfections. Gradually progress with higher grits (e.g. 400-600) for a smoother surface. Be sure to sand evenly and with gentle pressure to avoid damaging the resin

2. **Polishing:** Once you achieve a uniformly smooth surface, it is time to bring out the shine. Polishing compounds or diamond polishing pads are commonly used for this purpose. Apply the polishing compound to a soft cloth or pad and work it over the resin in circular motions. Continue with finer polishing compounds until you achieve the desired level of gloss and clarity.

Sealing and Protecting your Artwork

To ensure the longevity of your epoxy resin art, sealing and protecting it from environmental factors is crucial.

1. **Sealing:** After sanding and polishing, it is essential to seal the

surface to protect it from Ultra Violet (UV) radiation, which can cause epoxy resin to yellow or become brittle over time. Apply a UV-resistant clear coat or epoxy resin topcoat to shield your artwork from sunlight and other harmful elements.

2. **Framing:** Framing your epoxy resin art can provide an extra layer of protection. A well-designed frame can not only enhance the presentation of your artwork, but also serve as a barrier against dust, moisture, and physical damage.

3. **Display considerations:** When choosing a location to display your epoxy resin artwork, keep it away from direct sunlight, extreme temperature, and humidity. These environmental factors can accelerate resin degradation and discoloration.

Long Term Care and Maintenance

Preserving the beauty of your epoxy resin artwork requires ongoing care and maintenance.

1. **Regular cleaning:** Dust and debris can accumulate on the surface of

your artwork over time. Gently dust your piece with a soft, lint-free cloth or use a compressed air canister to remove debris from crevices and textured areas.

2. **Re-Sealing:** Over the years, the protective sealant may wear down. Periodically inspect your artwork, and if you notice any signs of damage or wear, consider reapplying a clear protective coat to maintain its integrity.

3. **Avoiding Impact:** Epoxy resin, while durable, can still be susceptible to physical damage. Be cautious when handling and moving your artwork to prevent scratches or cracks.

So, master the techniques of sanding, polishing, sealing, and proper care, and your epoxy resin creations will remain vibrant and beautiful for years to come. A well-maintained epoxy resin artwork can be a timeless piece that continues to captivate viewers and bring joy to its owner.

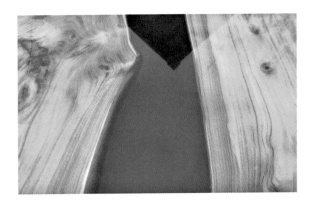

CHAPTER 6: Inspiration and Creativity

In this chapter, we will explore the process of nurturing your artistic identity and drawing inspiration from the world around you.

Developing Your Own Style

Every artist possesses a unique voice waiting to be discovered and honed. Developing your own style in epoxy resin art is a rewarding endeavor that allows you to leave a distinctive mark on the art world.

1. **Experimentation:** Begin by experimenting with different techniques, color palettes, and materials. Try various pouring methods, mixing inclusions, and exploring new textures. Through trial and error, you will discover what resonates with you and what sets your work apart.

2. **Self-Reflection:** Take the time to reflect on your artistic journey. Analyze your past creations and identify recurring themes or elements that you are particularly drawn to. Consider what emotions or messages you want to convey through your art.

3. **Consistency:** While experimentation is essential, consistency in certain aspects of your work can help define your style. This might include a particular color scheme, a signature technique, or a recurring motif that ties your creations together.

4. **Study Other Artists:** Study the work of other epoxy resin artists and artists from various disciplines. Observe their techniques, but also try to discern what it is about their work that resonates with you. This can provide valuable insights into your own artistic preferences.

5. **Seek Feedback:** Don't hesitate to seek feedback from peers, mentors, or art communities. Constructive criticism can help you refine your style and grow as an artist.

Inspiration from Nature and Everyday Life

Inspiration can be found everywhere, from the grandeur of nature to the simplicity of everyday life. Here are some ways to draw creative inspiration from your surroundings:

1. **Nature:** Nature is a boundless source of inspiration for epoxy resin artists. Study the intricate patterns of leaves, the colors of a sunset, or the textures of rocks. Incorporating elements of nature into your art can evoke a sense of tranquility and wander.

2. **Everyday life:** The ordinary can be extraordinary when viewed through an artistic lens. Explore the beauty in everyday objects, whether it is the play of light on a rain-soaked street, the arrangement of kitchen utensils, or the symmetry of architectural designs. These ordinary moments can spark unique ideas for your artwork.

3. **Emotions and Experiences:** Your own emotions and life experiences can be powerful catalysts for creativity. Channel your feelings, memories, and personal stories into your art. Your authenticity as an artist can resonate deeply with viewers.

4. **Travel and Cultural Experiences:** Traveling to new places and experiencing different cultures can broaden your perspective and provide fresh insights. Expose yourself to diverse

landscapes, traditions, and art forms to enrich your artistic vocabulary.

5. **Keep a Sketchbook:** Carry a sketchbook with you to capture fleeting moments of inspiration. Sketching and jotting down ideas can help you remember to develop concepts for future epoxy resin projects.

CHAPTER 7: Turning Your Art into a Business

For many epoxy resin artists, the dream of turning their passion into a successful business is both exciting and achievable. In this chapter, we will explore the essential steps and strategies to help you transform your epoxy resin art into a thriving enterprise.

Pricing and Selling Your Art

Determining the right price for your epoxy resin art is a critical step in establishing a successful art business. Here's how to navigate this important aspect:

1. Cost Calculation:

The first step in establishing a successful art business is to calculate the cost associated with creating each piece of epoxy resin artwork. This process involves a meticulous breakdown of expenses, including the cost of materials, labor, studio space, and any other overheads. It is vital to account for your own time and expertise as part of the cost calculation. This comprehensive approach ensures that you have a clear understanding of the financial investments in each piece.

2. Market Research:

In determining the right price for your epoxy resin art, thorough market research is essential. This research involves studying the pricing trends within the epoxy resin art market. Examine the prices of similar pieces created by other artists to gain insights into what the market can bear. Additionally, assess the demand for your specific artistic style and niche. Understanding the market dynamics will enable you to position your artwork competitively.

3. Pricing Strategy:

Selecting an effective pricing strategy is pivotal for your art business. Your pricing strategy should align with your brand identity and resonate with your target audience. There are various approaches you can consider:

- **Size-based Pricing:** Base your pricing on the size of your artwork. Larger pieces may command a higher price due to the increased materials and effort required.
- **Complexity-Based Pricing:** If your artworks vary in complexity, consider adjusting prices accordingly. More intricate pieces can justify a higher price tag.
- **Uniqueness:** The uniqueness of each artwork can also influence pricing. One-of-a-kind or limited-edition pieces may be priced higher to reflect their exclusivity.
- **Transparency:** Ensure transparency in your pricing structure. Clearly communicate the

factors that contribute to the cost of each piece so that customers understand the value they are receiving.

4. Multiple Revenue Streams:

To maximize your income potential as an epoxy resin artist, consider diversifying your revenue streams. While selling original artworks is a primary focus, there are several supplementary avenues to explore:

- **Prints:** Offer prints of your original artworks at various price points. This enables a broader range of art enthusiasts to access your work.
- **Merchandise:** Create merchandise featuring your art such as posters, clothing or home décor items. These products can appeal to a wider audience and generate additional income.
- **Custom commissions:** Accept custom commissions from clients who desire personalized epoxy resin pieces. Tailoring your art to individual preferences can be a lucrative endeavor.

5. Sales Platforms:

Selecting the right sales platforms is crucial for reaching your target audience. There are several options to consider:

- **Art Galleries:** Collaborate with art galleries to exhibit and sell your epoxy resin art. Galleries provide exposure to a diverse audience of art collectors.
- **Online Marketplaces:** Leverage online marketplaces such as Etsy, Shopify or others to showcase and sell your art. These platforms offer the advantage of a global reach.
- **Personal Website:** Create and maintain a professional artist website that features your portfolio and includes an integrated online store. A personal website provides you with full control over your brand and sales process.

Marketing Strategies for Artists

Marketing is a fundamental aspect of establishing a successful art business. It's the bridge that connects your creativity with potential buyers and art enthusiasts. Here, we will delve into some effective marketing strategies tailored to artists:

1. Branding

- **Brand Identity:** Your brand is more than just a logo; it encompasses your artistic style, values, and the unique story behind your art. Take some time to develop a strong brand identity that reflects who you are as an artist.
- **Consistency:** Ensure that your branding remains consistent across all your marketing materials, from your website to your social media profiles. Consistency helps in creating a memorable and cohesive brand image.

2. Social Media Presence

- **Platform Selection:** Choose the social media platforms that align with your target audience and artistic niche. Platforms like Instagram, Facebook and Pinterest are popular choices for artists.
- **Showcase Your Art:** Regularly post high-quality images of your artwork. Use engaging captions to provide context and insights into your creative process.
- **Behind-the-Scenes:** Share behind-the-scenes glimpses of your studio, work in progress, and the inspirations that drive your art. This

humanizes your brand and allows your audience to connect with you on a personal level.

- **Engagement:** Actively engage with your followers by responding to comments, participating in art-related discussions, and collaborating with other artists. Interaction fosters a sense of community around your art.

3.Email Marketing

- **Building an Email list:** Create an email list by inviting interested art enthusiasts and collectors to subscribe. You can collect email addresses through your website, social media, or art events.
- **Regular Newsletters:** Send out regular newsletters to your subscribers, featuring updates on your latest creation, upcoming exhibition, art-related news, and exclusive offers.
- **Personalization:** Tailor your email content to your audience's interests and preferences. Personalization helps foster a deeper connection with your subscribers.
- **Call to Action (CTA):** Include clear and compelling CTA's in your

emails. Encourage recipients to visit your website, make a purchase, or attend an art show.

4.Networking

- **Attend Art Events:** Participate in art exhibitions, fairs, and local events. Networking with fellow artists, art enthusiasts, and potential buyers can open doors to collaborations, commissions, and sales.
- **Art Communities:** Join online and local art communities where you can share your work, gain exposure, and learn from other artists. Networking within these communities can lead to valuable connections and opportunities.

5.Website and online store

- **Professional website:** Create a professional artist website that serves as a central hub for your online presence. Your website should showcase your portfolio, provide insights into your artistic journey, and offer contact information.
- **Online stores:** If you sell your art, integrate your online store into your

website for easy art purchases. Ensure that your online store is user-friendly, secure, and mobile responsive.

- **Blogging:** Consider maintaining a blog on your website where you can share in-depth articles about your art, techniques and experiences. Blogging not only informs but also helps improve your website's search engine visibility.

Building an Online Presence

In the digital age, having a strong online presence is vital for art businesses. Here's how to establish and enhance your online presence:

1. **Website Optimization:** Ensure your website is user-friendly, mobile-responsive, and optimized for search engines (SEO). This will make it easier for potential buyers to discover your art online.
2. **Content Creation:** Regularly update your website and social media channels with fresh content, including new artwork, blog posts and videos. Engaging content keeps

your audience interested and informed.

3. **Online Marketplaces:** Consider listing your art on reputable online art marketplaces like Saatchi Art or Artsy. These platforms can expose your work to a global audience of art collectors.

4. **Online Advertising:** Invest in online advertising, such as posts on Facebook or Google Ads to reach a wider audience. Target your ads to specific demographics and interests to maximize their effectiveness.

CONCLUSION

In our exploration of epoxy resin art, we have ventured into a realm where creativity knows no bounds. From the foundational techniques that form the basis of resin art to the advanced methods that allow for boundless experimentation, we have traversed a landscape of artistic possibilities.

One of the central themes we have explored is the importance of preserving the beauty and longevity of epoxy resin creations. Proper finishing techniques, including sanding, polishing, and sealing, are instrumental in ensuring that each piece maintains its allure over time.

We have also delved into the realm of inspiration, emphasizing the significance of cultivating a unique artistic style and drawing creative influence from diverse sources. Whether it is the serenity of nature, the simplicity of everyday life, or the depth of your own experiences, there is an abundance of inspiration waiting to be harnessed.

For those with aspirations of turning their epoxy resin art into a business, we have discussed essential strategies, including thoughtful pricing, effective marketing, and the establishment of a robust online presence. These elements are the building blocks of a successful art business that can help artists reach a wider audience and sustain their creative endeavors.

As we conclude this journey, it is essential to remember that art is a lifelong pursuit. The path of an epoxy resin artist is one of continuous growth and self-discovery. Embrace your creativity, persist through challenges, and stay connected with the art community. Your unique perspective and creations have the power to inspire, captivate, and leave a lasting impact on the world. Continue to explore, create, and share your passion, for your artistic journey is far from its end; it is an enduring odyssey of self-expression and discovery.

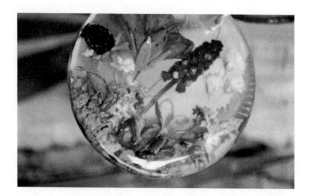

Made in the USA
Monee, IL
06 March 2024

54511797R00050